W9-BQV-395

# pocket posh
· · · · · · · · ·
# take care

## Inspired Activities
## for **Gratitude**

# pocket posh
· · · · · · · · · ·
# take care

## Inspired Activities
## for Gratitude

**Andrews McMeel**
PUBLISHING®

We all need some time to focus on ourselves. It's easy to become overwhelmed—by work, by home responsibilities, by the news of the day. It's important to step away, relax, and recenter. *Take Care: Inspired Activities for Gratitude* invites you to practice small moments of self-care through mindful activities, inspirational words, and thought-provoking journal prompts. Take some time for yourself.

. . . take care.

"Happiness is not a state
to arrive at, but a manner
of traveling."

—*Margaret Lee Runbeck*

```
R E C O G N I T I O N T J U I O U K O L
P Q L P J O P T I M I S T I C D O O N U
R T T O R I S P V N E H G I H E C U U C
A E R C M K P O O N Y N J Z B L H R U K
C I M E C U Z I O L I C D A W K E O G Y
T U S P O F T I L N T O N A R I E H I F
I U Y W Z A S U I O Z N W C D M R S V E
C Z L Z T S F L N Q O T S T N B F A E M
E A I I E E R Y O G I E I X J E U T T A
K G D R P E H F I N A N H B U N L I H P
E E P O V W B R I G H T S I D E C S A P
M X H L G U B L E S S E D O U F K F N R
E B I U P S U R K D I D C K P I I A K E
H S A S L F E T L Y C N S M B C A C S C
D P C A E C A A J X M E U M E I X T Q I
V Q N T N Y P R N Q H S I L A A M I T A
A T A I P O Q R W M C S G W T L H O Z T
B R S P G R A T I T U D E L I S T N X I
G E A D J V W C C O N S O L A T I O N O
O H T H A N K F U L A P L E A S E D O N
```

## attitude of gratitude

| | | |
|---|---|---|
| APPRECIATION | GONNA BE OK | PLEASED |
| BENEFICIAL | GRATEFUL | PRACTICE |
| BLESSED | GRATITUDE LIST | RECOGNITION |
| BRIGHT SIDE | HAPPY | SATISFACTION |
| CHEERFUL | HOPEFUL | SILVER LINING |
| CONSOLATION | LUCKY | SINCERE |
| CONTENTEDNESS | MEDITATION | THANKFUL |
| EXPRESSION | OM | UPBEAT |
| GIVE THANKS | OPTIMISTIC | WHY NOT |

3

# gratitude for today

Practicing gratitude is taking the time to be thankful
for the good things in our lives, and it has been
proven to improve emotional and physical health.
When we take the time to stop and appreciate what
we have, we reframe our perspective. Expressing
gratitude, even for the smallest things, can lead to
big change.

What are some things in your life that you are
grateful for today?

. . . . . . . . . . . . . . . . . . . . . . . . . . . . . . . . . . . . . . . . . . . . . . . .

. . . . . . . . . . . . . . . . . . . . . . . . . . . . . . . . . . . . . . . . . . . . . . . .

. . . . . . . . . . . . . . . . . . . . . . . . . . . . . . . . . . . . . . . . . . . . . . . .

. . . . . . . . . . . . . . . . . . . . . . . . . . . . . . . . . . . . . . . . . . . . . . . .

. . . . . . . . . . . . . . . . . . . . . . . . . . . . . . . . . . . . . . . . . . . . . . . .

. . . . . . . . . . . . . . . . . . . . . . . . . . . . . . . . . . . . . . . . . . . . . . . .

. . . . . . . . . . . . . . . . . . . . . . . . . . . . . . . . . . . . . . . . . . . . . . . .

# mindful gratitude exercise

Pick a physical object in your immediate vicinity
that you are grateful for. It could be something such
as a comfy chair, your favorite pen, or a treasured
keepsake. Take a few moments to think about what
this object means to you and how it might make
your life better. Does its color brighten your mood?
Does it have a nice smell? Does it remind you of
someone you love? No reason is too insignificant—
expressing appreciation for even the smallest things
is a key component of mindful gratitude. Over time,
practicing positive thinking like this can change your
perspective for the better.

"Optimism is a daily spiritual practice. And when we do it, we can transform this world."

—*Shawn Achor*

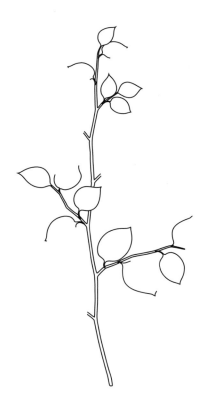

# Animals/Pets By Zhouqin Burnikel

## ACROSS

1. Place to dock or fish
5. Radar screen dot
9. L.L. Bean rival
11. Much-quoted Berra
12. Emotional support canine
14. Country where corn dogs and candy corn were invented
15. Jazz singer James
17. Place for a flag pin
19. Look over in a hurry
20. Once around the track
21. Sinking ship's signal
23. Chart-topper
24. Takes advantage of
26. ___ area (the sticks)
28. Job for a detective
29. "Kinda"
30. Emotional support equine
35. "Just Do It" company
36. "Speak of the devil," e.g.
37. Boatloads
38. ___ and flows

## DOWN

1. Post-bath wear, informally
2. Winter driving hazard
3. Make a blunder
4. Gun, as an engine
5. "Later!"
6. Rich ore deposits
7. "Makes sense"
8. Braided hairdo
10. Smartens (up)
13. Pepsi One has one
16. Pest at a picnic
17. Layered pasta dish
18. Hairy Halloween costume
20. Jean-___ Picard ("Star Trek" captain)
22. Dish often dipped in wasabi and soy sauce mixture
25. Ginza-based watchmaker
27. Providence, __ Island
31. Cub Scout group
32. ___ cage (chest protector)
33. Break down in tears
34. 911 response letters

"As you grow older,
you will discover that
you have two hands,
one for helping
yourself, the other
for helping others."

—*Sam Levenson*

```
N I E C E T L S I S T E R W C V S B J C
N U C H I L D R E N R M Y Y J O Y U Y M
E Y M F C E G A G E C H U S B A N D Y D
P Y F E O A X G H W T I R R O L P C G A
H C A A E Y O T R N P S P F V M I V R U
E G S M Z M O E U A K Z G R A N D M A G
W R P U X M H A V D N H F I T I P Q N H
D P V C D T R F U K B D H X M G T A D T
S R H O O V X F S Q T N S O U R L J D E
O Z G M D W D H J R X U G O R S Y G A R
N U C L E A R F A M I L Y P N Q B Z U L
T V C O U S I N T K P R B W A M J X G N
S I B L I N G X P I E G U R V A M I H Z
P S E M Q R K A H H D I K K V Z N S T Y
F C W Q P W P S T F A M I L Y T R E E U
G A F K P D N O U E E G Z X A M W K R E
P H T O N I R X L F Z C I F A T H E R I
D Q O A K B Y C I B N M G D M Y X D O I
K T R M T A N W G O D F A T H E R J F F
I G V J Q U N W I P W K P A R E N T I K
```

## family

| | | |
|---|---|---|
| BROTHER | GRANDDAUGHTER | NIECE |
| CHILDREN | GRANDMA | NUCLEAR FAMILY |
| COUSIN | GRANDPA | PARENT |
| DAUGHTER | GRANDSON | SIBLING |
| FAMILY TREE | HUSBAND | SISTER |
| FATHER | KINSHIP | SON |
| GODFATHER | MOTHER | UNCLE |
| GODMOTHER | NEPHEW | WIFE |

```
L Z L J F L U T E E E V
Y I K E Z L J C L N B X
V K O X M A H P U R N O
I O M N C M P J U Y L L
O N A V U A I M L L M E
L A N Y B C E N E Z A M
A I G G A L H C G X Y O
Z P O R G A N P E R U N
```

## find and circle

| | |
|---|---|
| Five mammals starting with "L" | ✓○○○○ |
| Five five-letter musical instruments | ○○○○○ |
| Three five-letter fruits | ○○○ |
| Two four-letter countries | ○○ |
| Two months | ○○ |

"Treasure the blessings
of an average day."

—*H. Jackson Brown, Jr.*

# start a gratitude journal

Spending a few minutes every day writing down the
things you're grateful for is a great habit to start.
Entries can be as short or as involved as you want—
a carefully composed essay about a loved one can be
as helpful as a three-item list of things that made
you happy today—but the key is consistency. "Choose
positivity" may sound trite, but regularly practicing
this kind of intentional positivity can take root in
your other thought patterns and interactions.
Give it a try!

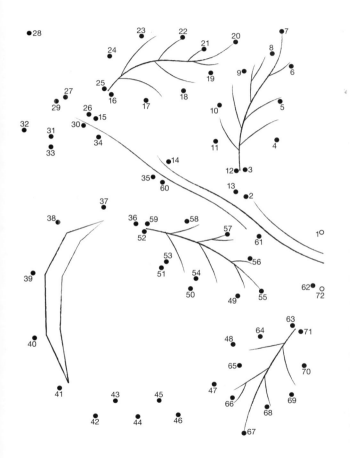

19

# counting ~~sheep~~ blessings

A good night's sleep starts with a good nighttime routine. Make gratitude an intentional component of your bedtime. A few minutes before you go to sleep, simply take some time to think about what you were grateful for that day. It's just as calming as counting sheep and much more emotionally rewarding.

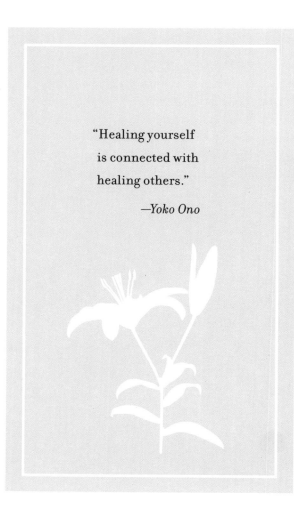

"Healing yourself
is connected with
healing others."

—*Yoko Ono*

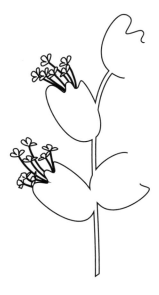

# creature comforts By Zhouqin Burnikel

## ACROSS

1. Not mincing words
6. Cheryl of "Charlie's Angels"
10. Search engine with an exclamation point in its logo
11. Okra field measures
13. Radiate, as confidence
14. Touch screen pens
15. Post-workout refresher
17. Efron of "The Greatest Showman"
18. Baptism or communion, e.g.
19. Relay race segment
22. Quid ___ quo
24. Lowest two-digit number
25. Knitting store purchase
27. Rival of FedEx
29. Post-workout relaxation spot
32. Tennis superstar Naomi
33. Popular question-and-answer website
36. Eye surgeon's beam
37. Called balls and strikes
38. Program that brings "ideas worth spreading" to local communities
39. Heroic tales

## DOWN

1. "See ya!"
2. Far from strict
3. "Forget it!"
4. Tablet that may help with an all-nighter
5. Line dance step
6. Mascara target
7. Stage performer
8. Deadpan humor
9. Strike out
12. Fire truck sound
16. Cancel, as a planned mission
19. Cleaning spray brand
20. Really bothers
21. Frying pan residue
23. Hard to see through
26. Like a skinny-dipper
28. Leave without an answer
30. "Das Kapital" author Karl
31. Tribe with kachina dolls
34. ___ room (play area)
35. Major revenue source for Google

"Happiness doesn't have to be chased . . . it merely has to be chosen."

—*Mandy Hale*

```
J O Y F U L A P Y O E J H B A C L X H X
K Y S Y X K Y G P T R L I V E L Y N X S
L B P O Y D S K A Y K P X B Q D K G B Q
N C R C L R E N O Z R L G L A D L P O T
B F K I C W U L B I U C H I R P Y L J H
B Q U U G T J A I F F E S T I V E D U R
Z L I Z R H Q F H G H J N H F T E G B I
N Q I O M J T T Y U H P A B H T V C I L
C P F T E Y R E A S T T P R N O A Y L L
E Y H Z H I O F X B H C E E U V L N A E
W B S I M E V V J U G G T D D E X Y N D
E I Y C H E E R F U L N N P X R K S T N
U S D H N E L E W V O T L I T J E D V Z
T X R B Z O X X C C F H A X J O B T C H
D R J E L A T E D S T V A N G Y U A H J
Q L I G H T H E A R T E D S T E S E I O
S A N V X D D U P B E A T A I D T K P Y
T K E P M E R R Y S U Z T S X H M B P O
P V N P L E A S E D W W Q I N R S X E U
J Q A X I I C S E S U N N Y C R O X R S
```

## happy adjectives

BLITHE
BRIGHT
CHEERFUL
CHIPPER
CHIRPY
CONTENTED
DELIGHTED
ECSTATIC
ELATED

EXULTANT
FESTIVE
FORTUNATE
GLAD
JOYFUL
JOYOUS
JUBILANT
LIGHTHEARTED
LIVELY

MERRY
MIRTHFUL
OVERJOYED
PLEASED
SUNNY
THRILLED
UPBEAT

# gratitude for connection

We all have people in our lives whose love and support make our lives better. Take a moment to think about them. Write down their names and what they mean to you. Try to reach out to these people in some way and express your feelings. Thinking about your appreciation for connection and community is a great way to practice gratitude, and actually nurturing those connections can have even greater benefits.

. . . . . . . . . . . . . . . . . . . . . . . . . . . . . . . . . . . . . . . .

. . . . . . . . . . . . . . . . . . . . . . . . . . . . . . . . . . . . . . . .

. . . . . . . . . . . . . . . . . . . . . . . . . . . . . . . . . . . . . . . .

. . . . . . . . . . . . . . . . . . . . . . . . . . . . . . . . . . . . . . . .

. . . . . . . . . . . . . . . . . . . . . . . . . . . . . . . . . . . . . . . .

. . . . . . . . . . . . . . . . . . . . . . . . . . . . . . . . . . . . . . . .

. . . . . . . . . . . . . . . . . . . . . . . . . . . . . . . . . . . . . . . .

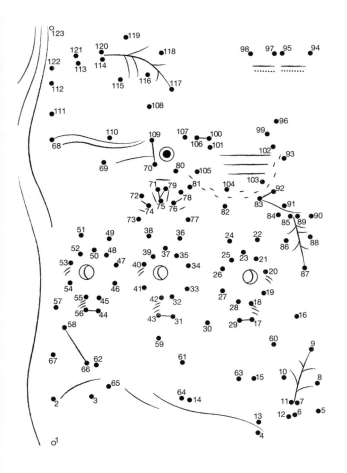

# journal prompt

There are so many timeless stories about gratitude, such as the fable about the lion with the thorn in his paw, the folktale about the crane wife, or the story of King Midas. Can you think of any that hold particular resonance for you? How did gratitude, or the lack of it, affect the stories' characters? Are there connective threads between the lessons of these stories and your own life?

. . . . . . . . . . . . . . . . . . . . . . . . . . . . . . . . . . . . . . . . . . .

. . . . . . . . . . . . . . . . . . . . . . . . . . . . . . . . . . . . . . . . . . .

. . . . . . . . . . . . . . . . . . . . . . . . . . . . . . . . . . . . . . . . . . .

. . . . . . . . . . . . . . . . . . . . . . . . . . . . . . . . . . . . . . . . . . .

. . . . . . . . . . . . . . . . . . . . . . . . . . . . . . . . . . . . . . . . . . .

. . . . . . . . . . . . . . . . . . . . . . . . . . . . . . . . . . . . . . . . . . .

. . . . . . . . . . . . . . . . . . . . . . . . . . . . . . . . . . . . . . . . . . .

"You're a diamond. Never sell yourself as coal."

—*Mina Rehman*

# Family Time By Zhouqin Burnikel

## ACROSS

1. Letters on a Coppertone bottle
4. Genre for Cardi B
7. Place for pillow talk
10. "__ be darned!"
11. Org. that monitors drinking water
12. Vowel's value in Scrabble
13. Enjoy a meal in the park
16. Promoted heavily
17. Stovetop appliance
18. Tie the knot
20. Moore of "Ghost"
21. Roam (about)
24. NBA whistle blower
26. Pic on a ankle, perhaps
27. "Planet of the ___"
29. Thumbs-down vote
31. Scratch-off ticket game
33. Pants with a skinny style
37. Toss a flying disc in the park, say
39. "Green Book" actor Mahershala ___
40. In good shape
41. Garment with an underwire
42. "OMG, that cracks me up!"
43. Place for a salt scrub
44. Podcast interruptions

## DOWN

1. World-weary exhalation
2. Devious tactic
3. Box office disaster
4. Book club member
5. Program activated with a finger tap
6. Two queens, e.g.
7. Baby hat often tied under the chin
8. Inscrutable sort
9. Scammer's forte
14. Right out of the box
15. Despicable guy
19. Room with a recliner
21. Ladies' night attendee
22. Storied Harlem theater
23. Micromanagement concern
25. Dish served in a sizzling skillet
28. Hog haven
30. "Absolutely!"
32. Trade-___ (concessions)
34. "Dancing Queen" band
35. Stereotypical techie
36. Large bodies of water
38. __ Van Winkle

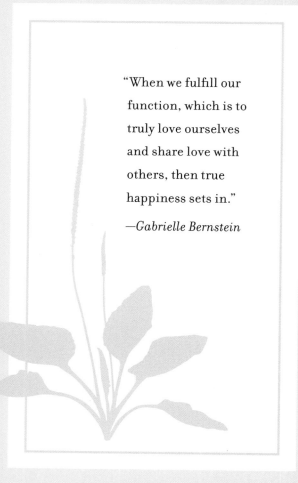

"When we fulfill our function, which is to truly love ourselves and share love with others, then true happiness sets in."

—*Gabrielle Bernstein*

```
A J F X Y P R O M O T I O N T U T C X W
L G N Y S J Y U B F W T X Y O Z D H Y I
S T P A T R I C K S S H A N X T F R M N
L M B Z E A S T E R N D V E F R J I A N
M L R X J U Q N A C S O F W F D N S R I
A H A T T M I E D T I Y L J Y T C T T N
R F O B O P Y Z N O I E M O Z J I M I G
R T O M O W N E W B A B Y B G L H A N G
I V W U E R D R V A L E N T I N E S L A
A U Q N R I D D J V O V S P N G U E U M
G G C B S T H A G R A D U A T I O N T E
E E L E D Z H J Y A Z K W A N Z A A H B
Y A R J U O H O R E T I R E M E N T E M
H P X W Z I E C F Q V A C A T I O N R Y
A W E E K E N D H J P Z M A Y D A Y K S
N D S O Y N U J X F U P I J A O Z P I U
U H A L L O W E E N M L U K N T S M N M
K V E T E R A N S D A Y Y A X I O I G M
A A C Z T H A N K S G I V I N G Z G I E
H F H K B B I R T H D A Y N T B B G E R
```

## time to celebrate

BIRTHDAY
CHRISTMAS
EASTER
FOURTH OF JULY
GRADUATION
HALLOWEEN
HANUKAH
LABOR DAY
KWANZAA

MARRIAGE
MARTIN LUTHER
  KING
MAY DAY
NEW BABY
NEW JOB
NEW YEAR'S
PRESIDENTS' DAY
PROMOTION

RETIREMENT
ST. PATRICK'S
SUMMER
THANKSGIVING
VACATION
VALENTINE'S
VETERANS DAY
WEEKEND
WINNING GAME

```
G V Z P X F L I P P E R
Z O A K E A A J B I J A
L P L L I D W C I L N V
T Z H D M E I T I I U K
E J N Y H O I C H A K E
A I A S Y A N C U Y L H
L R A Z H X J D X R K C
G C M A N I C U R E E B
```

## find and circle

| | |
|---|---|
| Five four-letter colors | ⦿○○○○ |
| Three spa services | ○○○ |
| Three five-letter countries | ○○○ |
| Two six-letter nuts | ○○ |
| Appendage for a whale or dolphin | ○ |

"The goal of life is to make your heartbeat match the beat of the universe, to match your nature with Nature."

—*Joseph Campbell*

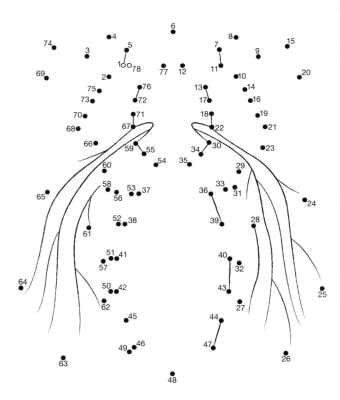

"Stand for something or you will fall for anything. Today's mighty oak is yesterday's nut that held its ground."

—*Rosa Parks*

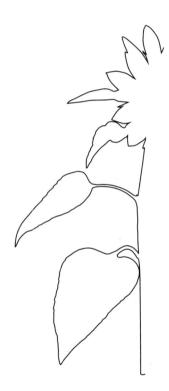

# Gratitude By Zhouqin Burnikel

## ACROSS

1. Wood for surfboard blanks
6. "Waterloo" singing group
10. False identity
11. Osso buco meat
12. Words of gratitude
14. Counterpart of paleo-
15. Lump of dirt
17. Treat with disdain
19. Long-eared hopper
20. "I finally get it now!"
21. Wimbledon unit
23. Band's vehicle
24. Minor fender damage
26. "Cosmos" author Carl
28. First Bond movie
29. "Full Frontal With Samantha Bee" channel
30. Words of gratitude
35. Went by plane
36. Refueling ship
37. On __ (in the middle of a winning streak)
38. Take the wheel

## DOWN

1. "Kapow!"
2. In the manner of
3. ___-Manuel Miranda ("Hamilton" creator)
4. Turn down an offer
5. Colorful fall bloomers
6. "Selma" director DuVernay
7. Seat in the park
8. Pastry made with phyllo dough
9. Election loser
13. Abraham Lincoln attribute
16. __ mother (Cub Scout leader)
17. County lawman
18. Ricotta-stuffed dessert
20. Go on to say
22. Forbidden topics
25. Ivory ___ (academia)
27. Astronaut's wear
31. Woolly mammal
32. Cheer for a bullfighter
33. Portia DeGeneres, ___ de Rossi
34. Drop the ball

"You get to define the
terms of your life."

—*Cheryl Strayed*

```
L C C C H E R R Y C H E E S E C A K E Y
P C L A H A L E M O N B A R S S E P G I
E A B V R R H U B A R B P I E I G N L É
A R Q A T A J S M O R E S S P M I O L R
N R E W N A M V I M H T E E U D N F C S
U O Q S F G N E T A L C U B D N F L H T
T T C M P Q E R L A Y G U U A U W V O R
B C L A L R A L M A N V P C O P A W C A
U A G R R T E A F I P H X S C E L Q O W
T K G X M A L S R O C P E Q U C N Y L B
T E E U R L M E S T O T L S X A U P A E
E X L M I P M E O O A D I E T N T O T R
R P U N N B C L L T M C K S P B U E R
P A A K O R S G O S A R O A Q I R N C Y
I V W M G R G C O R H Z U L K E O D U S
E G E G E V O O I A X A F F N E W C P O
R L C T P H R T H X U U K O F Z N A C R
B T T H C R È M E B R U L E E L I K A B
H U P E A C H C O B B L E R U V E E K E
B K K A P P L E C R I S P V Z D S S E T
```

## desserts

ANGEL FOOD CAKE
APPLE CRISP
BUTTERSCOTCH
  PUDDING
CANNOLI
CARAMEL APPLES
CARAMEL SHAKE
CARROT CAKE
CHERRY CHEESECAKE

CHOCOLATE
  CUPCAKE
CHOCOLATE SOUFFLÉ
CRÈME BRULEE
ESPRESSO TRUFFLES
LEMON BARS
LEMON MERINGUE PIE
PEACH COBBLER
PEANUT BUTTER PIE

PECAN PIE
PLUM TART
POUND CAKE
RHUBARB PIE
SMORES
STRAWBERRY SORBET
TIRAMISU
VANILLA MALT
WALNUT BROWNIES

# natural wonder

We often get so wrapped up in our everyday activities and responsibilities that it's easy to forget about the world outside of ourselves. Try to spend some time in nature when you can, but just thinking about the beauty of nature can provide benefits too. Spending time thinking about the natural world can cultivate a healthy sense of wonder and awe. Not only does it remind us that there is a world beyond our immediate to-do lists and problems, being mindful of the beauty that surrounds you can increase your appreciation for life.

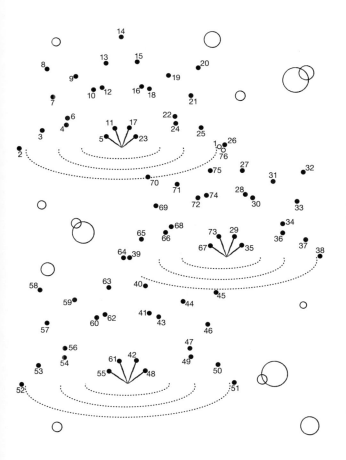

```
G P S Z C W I N D Y Y S
Y O I X L L E V E N R Y
R G L K U Z O K N E Y N
E H V D N K A U N X U O
T L E O C L S N D Z M N
S F R J H Z I J V Y M Y
Y B P O N D C O V E Y M
M B R E A K F A S T Z X
```

## find and circle

| | |
|---|---|
| Three Olympic medals | ⦿○○ |
| Three meals | ○○○ |
| Three words with two "Y"s | ○○○ |
| Three weather conditions ending in "Y" | ○○○ |
| Three four-letter bodies of water | ○○○ |

"What you do makes a difference, and you have to decide what kind of difference you want to make."

—*Jane Goodall*

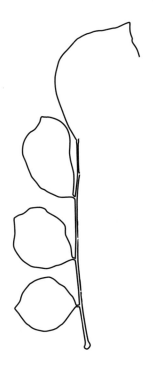

## HOLIDAYS By Zhouqin Burnikel

ACROSS

1. Croc's cousin
6. "Mamma Mia" singers
10. Food court enticement
11. Cross-promotional gimmick
12. Frozen daiquiri insert
13. Fitbit spot
14. Summer holiday
16. "A long long time ___ ..."
17. Free of contaminants
18. Insta image
21. Jazz band's job
23. ___ and Jerry
24. Per person
26. Do some quilting
28. Winter holiday
31. Cash, slangily
32. "Stop already!"
35. Really bother
36. "I'm serious!"
37. In apple-pie order
38. Covert ops acquisition

DOWN

1. Helium or hydrogen
2. Busts or murals
3. Civil wrong
4. Largest city in Nebraska
5. It's often cracked over a bowl of hot rice in Japan
6. Inflates, as tires
7. Largest city in Lebanon
8. Left Bank eatery
9. "O Canada" or "La Marseillaise"
11. ___-faced (duplicitous)
15. Impose (on)
18. Ghost-gobbling arcade game
19. Apple with apps
20. Dos Equis rival
22. Twins of the zodiac
25. Cockpit figure
27. Oregon Trail transport
29. "Come to think of it ..."
30. River delta deposit
33. Compete (for)
34. Slithery fish used in unadon

"Surround yourself with the dreamers, the doers, the believers and thinkers; but most of all surround yourself with those who see greatness within you even when you don't see it yourself."

*—Edmund Lee*

```
S  V  J  Z  C  E  L  L  O  K  X  B
X  O  K  U  O  R  L  A  N  D  O  E
R  B  D  W  I  M  I  A  M  I  Z  E
A  A  T  A  Z  C  S  N  A  K  E  R
T  N  A  T  H  D  E  U  C  E  V  K
I  J  M  E  A  L  I  Z  A  R  D  L
U  O  P  R  R  V  I  O  L  I  N  I
G  Z  A  B  P  C  K  W  I  N  E  M
```

## find and circle

| | |
|---|---|
| Six beverages (four-letter min.) | ⬤○○○○○ |
| Five stringed instruments | ○○○○○ |
| Three Florida cities | ○○○ |
| Two reptiles | ○○ |
| Card with two pips | ○ |

65

"We can choose to be affected
by the world or we can choose
to affect the world."

—Heidi Wills

```
K M S U S A N W O J C I C K I I Q D U A
N H E L E N C L A R K E F C H T U T G N
G A I L K E L L Y P P J R E D M E Q X G
Q Z R O I J A N E T Y E L L E N E B E E
G D Y M P N W M X L Y Q E C L B N J L L
B U D G B J D Z A A Q F X A L Q E M L I
V B K D V H G A M R N W C T H O L I E N
N M E E W N I A G E Y S J F X R I C N A
O A J Y I A S L S A A B N K A F Z H D J
P H N H O S N O L P T A A H T I A E E O
R J C C I N R N Y A H E H R I L B L G L
A O O R Y E C M A C R C S Y R Z E L E I
H A A Y N P A E T W O Y O J T A T E N E
W M M E C U E E K K I O C A O J H O E X
I N R Y L E R L A N N N C L C X I B R L
N I M X H A B D O A O A T X I C I A E N
F U M O G O N A R S R W S O W N O M S X
R C E R K A O D N F I S L F U S T A F S
E J A Y H M N D A D Z K S E P R C O F L
Y M O C O I L S F X A O G V S N H E N P
```

## influential women

AMY HOOD

AMY PASCAL

ANGELINA JOLIE

ANNA WINTOUR

BEYONCÉ
KNOWLES

CHANDA
KOCHHAR

ELLEN DEGENERES

GAIL KELLY

HELEN CLARK

HILLARY CLINTON

HO CHING

INDRA NOOYI

IRENE ROSENFELD

JANET YELLEN

JOYCE BANDA

MARGARET CHAN

MARISSA MAYER

MARY BARRA

MELINDA GATES

MICHELLE OBAMA

NANCY PELOSI

OPRAH WINFREY

QUEEN ELIZABETH II

SAFRA CATZ

SUSAN WOJCICKI

## find and circle

| | |
|---|---|
| Four mammals starting with "L" | ⊘○○○ |
| Four seven-letter jobs | ○○○○ |
| Three countries containing "Z" | ○○○ |
| Clue | ○ |
| Burial chamber | ○ |

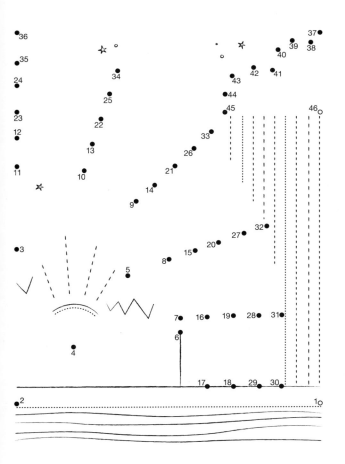

# thanksgiving every day

Thanksgiving is about being grateful for life's abundance. But you don't have to be sitting down to a holiday feast to appreciate your food. Many faith traditions have explicit practices around this, for instance saying a prayer of thanks before a meal. But you don't have to be faithful to be thankful—taking a moment to reflect before you eat provides occasion to practice both mindfulness and gratitude.

"You don't have to like everybody, but you have to love everybody."

—*Fannie Lou Hamer*

| R | Y | L | P | W | W | Y | P | A | R | I | S |
| T | O | K | I | A | E | Z | J | N | P | N | A |
| S | P | M | S | S | N | S | I | B | R | E | T |
| A | G | R | E | O | B | L | T | E | O | U | H |
| E | A | Z | D | V | R | O | Y | U | T | T | E |
| W | Z | N | W | E | E | K | N | R | O | R | N |
| X | O | K | B | P | E | S | O | O | N | O | S |
| L | M | A | D | R | I | D | J | V | K | N | Z |

## find and circle

| | |
|---|---|
| Eight European capitals | ⊘○○○○○○○ |
| Two parts of an atom | ○○ |
| Two opposing directions | ○○ |
| Two four-letter currencies | ○○ |
| Seven-day time period | ○ |

"Hopeful thinking can get you out of your fear zone and into your appreciation zone."

—Martha Beck

# nourishment By Zhouqin Burnikel

## ACROSS

1. Fawn's mom
4. ___ Four (the Beatles)
7. Thumbs-up vote
10. One of two in a rowboat
11. In the past
12. Publish personal information online to discredit someone
13. Homemade flu remedy
16. Soft jacket material
17. Like Loki and Thor
18. Sis or bro
20. Oktoberfest beverage
21. Lamb's mom
24. "What's the ___?" ("Who cares?")
26. Stage construction
27. Deli counter call
29. Maidenform garment
31. Slurpee alternatives
33. "Shucks!"
37. Leafy dinner course
39. "The A-Team" muscleman
40. Fitting
41. Put into practice
42. Billboard displays
43. "___ Doubtfire"
44. Diver's perfect score

## DOWN

1. ER workers
2. Diamond Head's island
3. Lake near Niagara Falls
4. Fraudulent driver's license, e.g.
5. "Act your ___!"
6. Capital of West Germany
7. Loves to pieces
8. "Here's the thing ..."
9. Authority on a subject
14. Jewel box contents
15. Weep audibly
19. Baby's mealtime neckwear
21. Total mystery
22. Convenience store sign
23. Puts forth, as pressure
25. Puts the icing on the cake
28. ___ Talks (online lecture series)
30. "I see it now!"
32. Stitching on a softball
34. Market surplus
35. Lack of hassles
36. Biblical paradise
38. "Morning Edition" network

"Whatever anybody says or does, assume positive intent. You will be amazed at how your whole approach to a person or problem becomes very different."

—Indra Nooyi

```
G G A Z E L L E C Y T A
K O O M A T H E N R I L
L R A R Z X F O E O B U
I U S T I F I H L T I B
B M I V A L P V Y S A I
R E A R J O L H N I B F
E F I J G K C A X H C H
G G I B B O N B K G N U
```

## find and circle

| | |
|---|---|
| Eight mammals starting with "G" | ⊘○○○○○○○ |
| Three human bones | ○○○ |
| Two school subjects | ○○ |
| Two felines starting with "L" | ○○ |
| Largest continent | ○ |

# gratitude box

Physically writing things down can make thoughts
feel more real. Take it a step further. Create a
gratitude box where you can store your appreciation.
When you think of something you're grateful for,
write it down on a slip of paper and put it in your
gratitude box. Set aside a specific date in the future
(maybe your next birthday, maybe next New Year's
Eve), sit down with your box, and read through what
you've written. Immersing yourself in months' or
years' worth of blessings, big and small, is bound to
make you feel even more grateful.

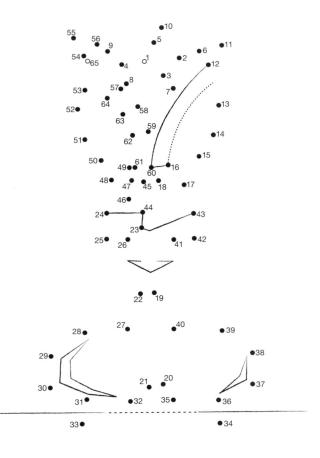

"We're here for a reason.
I believe a bit of the
reason is to throw little
torches out to lead people
through the dark."

—*Whoopi Goldberg*

# grateful for you

We often aren't as kind to ourselves as we should be.
It's easy to be your own toughest critic, but we all
have our own unique gifts and strengths that make
the world richer. Think about that list of people
you're grateful for that you made earlier. Now
think about who might put *you* on their gratitude
list. Think about yourself from someone else's
perspective. Why might they be grateful for you?
Write these thoughts down and refer back to them
the next time you're feeling down about yourself.

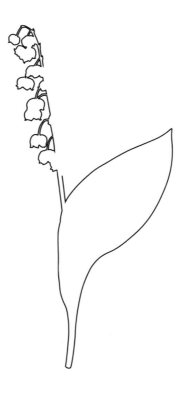

# SPIRITUALITY By Zhouqin Burnikel

## ACROSS

1. Mount Olympus residents
5. Desktop seen at the Genius Bar
9. Revises an Instagram post
11. ___ Scotia
12. Practice of mindfulness
14. Instagram chuckle
15. Read, as a QR code
17. Helicopter part
19. Gift wrapper's roll
20. Maple tree yield
21. Boxer or beagle
23. Morning moisture
24. Harbor strolling place
26. "Well done!"
28. Paquin of "True Blood"
29. ___ Lilly (pharmaceutical giant)
30. Goal of 12-Across
35. Scrapped, as a launch
36. Spray 'n Wash target
37. "The Voice" coach Stefani
38. Fish prized for its roe

## DOWN

1. Precious stone
2. "___ to Joy"
3. Served, as time
4. Clown's walking stick
5. Bank acct. addition
6. Like a fresh pumpkin bread
7. Creamy toast topper
8. Bite-sized sandwiches
10. Prepared to sing the national anthem
13. "Today" weather anchor
16. ___ Hampshire
17. Coming down in buckets
18. Post-renovation store sign
20. Five-star hotel feature
22. Takes a big swig
25. Free-___ turkeys
27. Keto and Paleo, for two
31. Geological time span
32. Hot tub utterance
33. Org. based in Langley, Virginia
34. Come to a conclusion

"Be careful how you
are talking to yourself
because you are
listening."

—*Lisa Hayes*

```
C  B  F  I  R  S  T  J  B  S  M  E
E  O  J  Z  E  X  P  Z  S  U  C  N
N  K  N  O  O  E  J  E  I  M  O  O
O  N  B  E  N  N  N  L  U  P  A  G
B  O  V  O  V  I  E  R  J  H  C  K
V  N  T  Z  S  H  D  A  R  T  H  V
K  E  J  U  H  Y  D  R  O  G  E  N
H  K  B  T  U  B  A  V  L  O  N  E
```

## find and circle

| | |
|---|---|
| Seven four-letter words ending in "ONE" | ⊘○○○○○○ |
| Three airline flight classes | ○○○ |
| Three four-letter musical instruments | ○○○ |
| The two lightest gases | ○○ |
| ____ Vader | ○ |

"Keep your face always towards
the sunshine, and the shadows
will fall behind you."

—*M.B. Whitman*

```
C C A M N N E B R O W N I E F U D G E E
H O A J I A E A Q A D P S C O O P S K D
A S O R X N T A C J I Z X D N Q F U N L
A P Q K A C T G P H V N F V M S Y O B C
C R U A I M T C C O A M Q B U U M R U O
H I P N J E E O H E L W P D I L P O T O
O N U E A F S L B O R I Y H A S N C T K
C K B T A S R A D E C I T O T T E K E I
O L M U E C L E N E I O I A V R U Y R E
L E Z R T L H O N D L H L E N A S R A D
A S P Y I T C E K C C I Z A W W D O L O
T S N N I R E Z S A H R G R T B B A M U
E H A P A F M R T A L V E H B E C D O G
C V L G F G N S P B N P A A T R C F N H
H N U O B Q I S O E A D G N M R I H D S
I S C S X P W R S F C N C R I Y Y A I J
P F R E N C H S I L K A A R X L X I X P
O Q W A F F L E C O N E N N E I L S T R
C H O C O L A T E F U D G E A A E A L P
Q C W D A L M O N D F U D G E K M V L G
```

## ice cream treat

ALMOND FUDGE
BANANA
BROWNIE FUDGE
BUTTER ALMOND
BUTTER PECAN
CARAMEL DELIGHT
CHOCOLATE CHIP
CHOCOLATE FUDGE
COFFEE

COOKIE DOUGH
COOKIES AND
  CREAM
ESPRESSO CHIP
FRENCH SILK
FRENCH VANILLA
MINT CHOCOLATE
  CHIP
NEAPOLITAN

PEACHES AND
  CREAM
PISTACHIO ALMOND
ROCKY ROAD
SCOOPS
SPRINKLES
STRAWBERRY
SUGAR CONE
VANILLA BEAN
WAFFLE CONE

"I think the best role
   models for women
   are people who are
   fruitfully and confidently
   themselves, who bring
   light into the world."

   —*Meryl Streep*

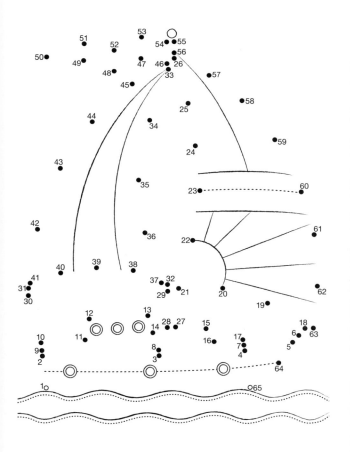

# pay it forward

One of the most effective ways to boost feelings of
satisfaction and well-being is to give back. Take
some time to identify a few causes you care about.
It doesn't have to be a complex global issue; it can be
something as simple as supporting your local library.
Get involved in whatever way makes sense for your
life, whether that means spreading awareness,
providing monetary support, or volunteering your
time. Share the positivity around.

"Learn to enjoy every minute of your life. Be happy now. Don't wait for something outside of yourself to make you happy in the future."

—*Earl Nightingale*

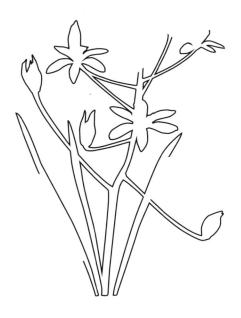

# Traveling/Trips By Zhouqin Burnikel

## ACROSS

1. Reason for extra innings
4. Stomach, to a tot
7. Spot on a domino
10. "Hmm, that's strange"
11. ___ Today (newspaper since 1982)
12. Golden years fund
13. Getaway for the meditative type
16. Got some shuteye
17. Implicitly understood
18. Yellowstone Park grazer
20. Cuban currency
21. "___ Town Road"
24. Item in an Easter basket
26. Bear cub's home
27. Burr-Hamilton contest
29. Step up to the plate
31. Bert's Muppet buddy
33. Vision correction surgery
37. Getaway for the outdoor type
39. "Told you so!"
40. Kenny G's instrument
41. Four's square root
42. "Just ___ water"
43. Give it a go
44. Enjoy a blueberry muffin

## DOWN

1. Playroom pieces
2. Person with a big Instagram following
3. Competitive advantage
4. Terrarium pet
5. "___ only as directed"
6. Damon of "True Grit"
7. Put (together)
8. Statement that may lead to folds
9. Stand-up comedian Oswalt
14. Chimp or gorilla
15. Nicki Minaj's music
19. Soviet spy org. in Bond movies
21. Major Black Sea port
22. Visited a forum often but never commented
23. Turned down
25. Samsung smart watch line
28. Tyler of "The Lord of the Rings"
30. Skin ink, slangily
32. Far ___ (Marco Polo's destination)
34. Destination often bookmarked
35. State with more hogs than humans
36. Shoelace mishap
38. Uber driver's need

"When you can't find your purpose in a day, make it to look after yourself."

—*Dodie Clark*

# notes

# notes

....................................................

....................................................

....................................................

....................................................

....................................................

....................................................

....................................................

....................................................

....................................................

....................................................

....................................................

....................................................

solutions

# SOLUTIONS

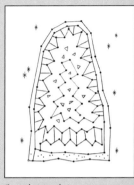

3    word search

5    dot to dot

10    spot the differences

12    crossword

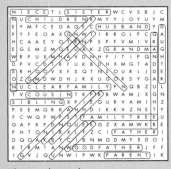

15   word search

LEMMING, LLAMA,
LEMUR, LYNX, LION—
VIOLA, PIANO, FLUTE,
ORGAN, CELLO—
APPLE, LEMON,
MANGO—CUBA,
PERU—JUNE, MAY

16   word roundup

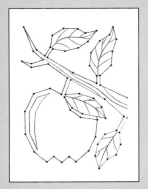

19   dot to dot

24   spot the differences

26  crossword

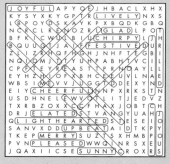

29  word search

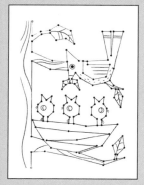

31  dot to dot

36  spot the differences

## 38 crossword

| S | P | F |   | R | A | P |   | B | E | D |
|---|---|---|---|---|---|---|---|---|---|---|
| I | L | L |   | E | P | A |   | O | N | E |
| G | O | O | N | A | P | I | C | N | I | C |
| H | Y | P | E | D |   | R | A | N | G | E |
|   |   |   | W | E | D |   | D | E | M | I |
| G | A | D |   | R | E | F |   | T | A | T |
| A | P | E | S |   | N | A | Y |   |   |   |
| L | O | T | T | O |   | J | E | A | N | S |
| P | L | A | Y | F | R | I | S | B | E | E |
| A | L | I |   | F | I | T |   | B | R | A |
| L | O | L |   | S | P | A |   | A | D | S |

## 41 word search

## 42 word roundup

GOLD, TEAL, BLUE,
GRAY, PINK—
MANICURE, PEDICURE,
FACIAL—INDIA, CHINA,
HAITI—CASHEW,
ALMOND—FLIPPER

## 44 dot to dot

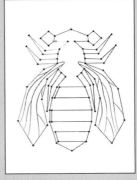

117

# SOLUTIONS

48 spot the differences

| B | A | L | S | A | | | A | B | B | A | |
| A | L | I | A | S | | | V | E | A | L | |
| M | A | N | Y | T | H | A | N | K | S | |
| | | | N | E | O | | C | L | O | D | |
| | S | C | O | R | N | | H | A | R | E | |
| A | H | A | | S | E | T | | V | A | N | |
| D | E | N | T | | S | A | G | A | N | |
| D | R | N | O | | T | B | S | | | |
| | I | O | W | E | Y | O | U | O | N | E |
| F | L | E | W | | | O | I | L | E | R |
| F | I | R | E | | | S | T | E | E | R |

50 crossword

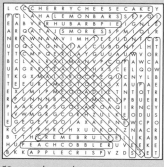

53 word search

55 dot to dot

118

BRONZE, SILVER, GOLD—BREAKFAST, DINNER, LUNCH—MYSTERY, SYNONYM, YUMMY—CLOUDY, SUNNY, WINDY—POND, LAKE, COVE

57 word roundup

60 spot the differences

62 crossword

WATER, JUICE, SODA, BEER, MILK, WINE—VIOLIN, GUITAR, CELLO, BANJO, HARP—ORLANDO, TAMPA, MIAMI—LIZARD, SNAKE—DEUCE

65 word roundup

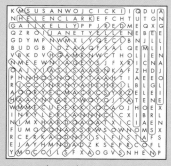

67 word search

LEMUR, LLAMA, LION,

LYNX—BUTCHER,

TEACHER, PLUMBER,

PAINTER—SWITZERLAND,

BRAZIL, ZAMBIA—

HINT—TOMB

68 word roundup

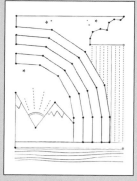

69 dot to dot

WARSAW, LONDON,

BERLIN, LISBON,

MADRID, ATHENS, PARIS,

ROME—NEUTRON,

PROTON—EAST, WEST—

PESO, EURO—WEEK

74 word roundup

# SOLUTIONS

76 spot the differences

78 crossword

| D O E | | F A B | | A Y E |
|---|---|---|---|---|

GORILLA, GIRAFFE,
GAZELLE, GIBBON,
GOPHER, GERBIL,
GOAT, GNU—FIBULA,
TIBIA, FEMUR—HISTORY,
MATH—LION, LYNX—
ASIA

81 word roundup

83 dot to dot

121

# SOLUTIONS

88  spot the differences

## 90 crossword

| G | O | D | S |   |   | I | M | A | C |
| E | D | I | T | S |   | N | O | V | A |
| M | E | D | I | T | A | T | I | O | N |
|   |   |   | L | O | L |   | S | C | A | N |
|   | R | O | T | O | R |   | T | A | P | E |
| S | A | P |   | D | O | G |   | D | E | W |
| P | I | E | R |   | K | U | D | O | S |   |
| A | N | N | A |   | E | L | I |   |   |   |
|   | I | N | N | E | R | P | E | A | C | E |
|   | N | O | G | O |   | S | T | A | I | N |
|   | G | W | E | N |   |   | S | H | A | D |

CONE, BONE, LONE,
GONE, NONE, TONE,
ZONE—BUSINESS, FIRST,
COACH—OBOE, TUBA,
DRUM—HYDROGEN,
HELIUM—DARTH

93  word roundup

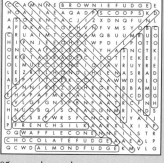

95  word search

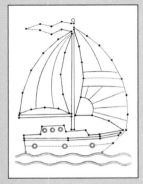

97 dot to dot

102 spot the differences

104 crossword

108 spot the differences

*Pocket Posh® Take Care: Inspired Activities for Gratitude*
copyright © 2020 by Andrews McMeel Publishing.
All rights reserved. Printed in China. No part of this
book may be used or reproduced in any manner
whatsoever without written permission except in
the case of reprints in the context of reviews.

Andrews McMeel Publishing
a division of Andrews McMeel Universal
1130 Walnut Street, Kansas City, Missouri 64106

www.andrewsmcmeel.com

20 21 22 23 24 RLP 10 9 8 7 6 5 4 3 2 1

ISBN: 978-1-5248-6056-1

Editor: Allison Adler
Art Director: Julie Barnes
Production Editor: Dave Shaw
Production Manager: Tamara Haus

**ATTENTION: SCHOOLS AND BUSINESSES**
Andrews McMeel books are available at quantity
discounts with bulk purchase for educational,
business, or sales promotional use. For information,
please e-mail the Andrews McMeel Publishing
Special Sales Department: specialsales@amuniversal.com.